Be Your Awesome Self

Mimi Novic

Aspiring Hope Publishing

Copyright © Mimi Novic 2024

All Rights Reserved. No part of this publication may be reproduced, stored in a retrieval system, or transmitted in any form or by any means, electronic, mechanical, photocopy, recording or otherwise, without prior written permission of the copyright owner.
Nor can it be circulated in any form of binding or cover other than that in which it is published and without similar condition including this condition being imposed on a subsequent purchaser.

British Library Cataloguing Publication Data.
A Catalogue record for this book is available from the British Library.

ISBN 978-1-0686848-4-5

Published by Aspiring Hope Publishing

With thanks to Artist Lynda Smith for the images

This Book Is Raising Funds For The Prince's Trust & KidsOut Charity

About The Author:

Mimi Novic is one of today's bestselling inspirational authors and is ranked amongst the top names in inspirational, motivational and spiritual books in the world. Her writings and quotes are considered some of the most popular in modern times and are used by some of today's most well known and influential figures.
She is internationally known as one of the most respected and highly regarded motivational and self awareness teachers in the fields of self-development. Her expertise has made her amongst the most popular and highly demanded well being experts of today.
Working as a complementary medical practitioner, psychotherapist, self development teacher, voiceover artist, author and motivational speaker her collaborations with renowned experts across various disciplines underscore her commitment to delivering unparalleled experiences in personal growth.
Mimi has collaborated with the most esteemed therapists, composers, musicians, professors, healers and professionals in their field while bringing together powerful teams that work in synchronicity to bring the best possible life enhancing experiences for her patients and clients.
She is known for her work with high profile personalities and her engagements with notable and influential figures further attest to her ability to navigate the intersections of success and wellness.
She teaches and runs workshops and seminars in a wide array of therapies, complementary medicine and self-awareness, working around the world in clinics, retreats and on a one to one basis.

Dear Dreamers & Believers

Welcome to your own world of wonderful wonder and amazement.
This is your journey and as you begin to read this book, on each page you are reminded how special you are, encouraging you to spread the beauty and kindness that is within you and make the world a better place.
It is filled with delightful thoughts and heartwarming quotes.
It contains within it jewels of wisdom, sprinkled with happiness dust, to light up your days and soothe your soul.
Whether it's the gentle whisper of the wind, the soothing song of bird, the smile of a friend, the raindrops in the sunlight, these lovely thoughts are here to show you the magic in everyday moments.
So, open your heart, and let these words take you on a journey where dreams come true, and love and joy are your guides.
May these pages inspire you to see the world with wonder and embrace the endless possibilities that life holds, while being courageous to be who you truly are.

With Love & Light
God Bless

Mimi Novic

YOUR DREAMS ARE THIS WAY

Beautiful moments are the special times that make us feel happy and loved. They can be as simple as a hug from a friend, a sunny day walking in the park, or sharing smiles and cake with special people.
These times remind us how wonderful life can be and fill our days with gladness.

Beautiful Moments

ARE ALWAYS MORE SPECIAL WHEN YOU ARE WITH SOMEONE YOU LOVE

YOU MUST TRUST YOURSELF AND KNOW THAT YOU
ARE SPECIAL JUST THE WAY YOU ARE.
BE BRAVE AND KEEP GOING EVEN WHEN THINGS
ARE NOT EASY.
EVERY SINGLE ONE OF US HAS SOMETHING TO
OFFER, AND BEING YOURSELF IS THE BEST THING
YOU CAN EVER BE.
TRUST IN YOUR ABILITIES, BE PROUD OF YOUR
TALENTS AND KNOW THAT YOU CAN ACHIEVE
GREAT THINGS JUST BY BEING YOU.

Have Belief In Who You Are

BE WHO YOU TRULY ARE AND YOU CAN
CONQUER ANYTHING

Imagine a world where everyone looked the same, acted the same and liked the same things. It would be pretty boring. Thankfully, everyone is different. Each person has unique gifts, interests and ways of seeing the world.

These differences make our world more colourful and exciting.

Whether it's the way you Smile, the music you love, or the way you sing, being different is what makes you special.

celebrate your uniqueness and never forget that it's our differences that make us all interesting in our own way.

Everyone Is Different

You are unique in your own way that's what makes you beautiful

Being strong means having the courage to face challenges and the determination to keep trying, even when things don't go as we planned. It's all about knowing you have a huge potential to overcome the most difficult obstacles and not giving up, no matter what happens.
Strength isn't just about physical power, it's also about being a thoughtful person and reaching out to others, while staying positive. everyone has their own powerful qualities that make them unstoppable.

You Are Strong

WHAT MAKES YOU POWERFUL IS THAT YOU NEVER STOP TRYING

Happiness begins with you.
It starts by finding joy in the little things you love and being grateful for what you have. When you're happy, it's like having an illuminated bright light inside you that shines and makes others around you feel lucky to know you.
By sharing your smiles, loveliness and laughter, you can show your personality to everyone you meet.
If you are content, you make this world better for others and yourself.

Happiness Begins With You

Being happy with yourself, means you can share your happiness with others

Finding a true friend feels like discovering a treasure. It's wonderful to have someone who understands you, shares time with you and makes you laugh loudly,
they are there to support you when you're sad and celebrate with you when you're enjoying good times.
Together you create fun, memories and enjoy the kind of adventures that bring a warm feeling. Having a friend like this makes you feel loved and cherished and it makes every day brighter.

Feeling Lovely

THERE IS A MAGICAL FEELING DEEP INSIDE OF YOU WHEN YOU FIND A TRUE FRIEND

Your journey is important because your inner light, the special spark inside you, belongs to you and shows you the right way when you feel lost. Just like a lantern shining brightly in the dark, your luminosity helps you to make good and positive choices,
be nice to yourself and others. Every step you take and every new thing you learn makes you shine even brighter, showing you the brilliant things you can do and the wonderful person you are becoming. Always believe in better and you will be on the right path, letting it lead you on your exciting adventures.

Your Journey Matters

Your inner light will always guide you towards the right path

Everything is possible.
When you believe, you can achieve amazing things, no matter how big or small.
It's like having a superpower that helps you reach for the moon and stars. Whether it's learning a new skill, making new friends, or solving a problem, believing and having faith gives you the strength and courage to keep walking towards your highest goals.
Always remember, you can do anything you set your mind to.

Believe

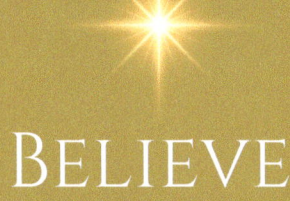

Everything is possible when you believe in your dreams

Do you know something fabulous?
if you Trust your soul you won't lose your way. Inside you, there's a special voice that knows what's right and helps you make good choices. It's like having a wise, friend who always looks out for you.
When you listen carefully, it helps you through tough times and helps you stay true to who you are.
Even if things get confusing or hard, trusting your soul will keep you happy and you can find the right path which will lead you to wonderful places.

Trust Your Soul

And you will never lose your way

When we have hope, it's like having a set of wings that lift us up and helps us soar above any challenges we face.

Hope makes us believe that marvellous things can happen, even when times are difficult and we think they will never end. It fills our heart with excitement and courage, pushing us to keep trying and never give up.

With hope by our side, we can reach for our dreams and fly higher than we ever thought possible. Every second we get another chance to try again.

Hope Gives Us Wings

NEVER GIVE UP THERE IS ALWAYS SOMETHING TO BE HOPEFUL ABOUT

Words matter when you speak from your heart. When you share your thoughts and feelings honestly, it helps others understand you better and brings you closer together. Speaking truly means being charitable, truthful and thoughtful with what you say. It shows that you care and makes people feel valued and loved. Your words have the power to make a big difference, so always let them come from a place of love and honesty.

Your Words Matter

When you speak from your heart everyone understands your words

Don't compare yourself to others because you are truly exceptional just as you are. Everyone has their own special talents and qualities. When you focus on being the best version of yourself, you can discover and celebrate all the wonderful things that make you a fabulous human being.
The world needs you as you are, one of a kind. Be assured of who you are and keep being your spectacular self.

Don't Compare

YOU ARE AMAZING JUST AS YOU ARE

Belonging in the right place means being where you feel accepted and valued for who you are. It's like finding a puzzle piece that fits perfectly, creating a sense of comfort and happiness.

When you feel that you belong, it is always when you are with people who appreciate and support you, making you feel safe and understood. the right place is where you can be your true self and know that you are important and where your heart feels at home and peaceful.

Belonging

You know when you are in the right place
when you feel at peace

Keep being brave, and you will always be a person who will have success. Being brave means trying new things, standing up for what is right and not ever giving up, even when things are tough. When you face your challenges with courage, you learn and grow stronger, opening the door to new opportunities. Bravery helps you overcome obstacles and discover anything is possible. So keep your head up and be strong. No matter what comes your way, your bravery will be your companion throughout your life.

Keep Being Brave

Keep doing what is right and every day will be an adventure

Your smile is like a ray of sunshine that can brighten up your day and make others feel happy to be around you.
When you smile, it lifts your spirits, making you feel more cheerful and less worried about stressful things.
When people see you being cheerful, it makes them smile, as you spread blessings wherever you go. These simple gestures can turn a bad day into a good one, help make new friends, and show others that you care.
No one else has your exceptional gift, so go and share it everywhere.

Smile

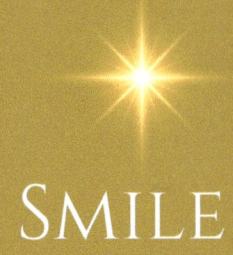

You bring sunshine wherever you go and make the clouds of sadness dissappear

Kindness begins with you because it starts with your own choices and what you do with them as a person.
When you let yourself be kind, you can do things like listening to a friend, helping someone in need, or simply being patient and understanding.
These small acts can make a big difference, not only in someone else's day but also in your own life. It creates a sense of connection and makes us feel sincere.
When others feel your care, they're inspired to act kindly also, this makes a ripple effect happen that can positively impact each person you meet.

Kindness Begins With You

BEGIN TO BE KIND TO YOURSELF AND YOU WILL ALSO BRIGHTEN SOMEONE ELSE'S DAY

Being positive is about taking small steps every day that bring you closer to your dreams and goals. This can mean reading, visiting friends, practising something you love, or just being gentle to yourself and all those you meet.

When you focus on joyful things, even the little ones, you build a pathway to reaching what makes you happy.

Every day offers a new opportunity to make progress and by staying optimistic, you will find yourself moving steadily but surely towards your wishes.

Be Positive

![illustration]

Do something everyday that brings you closer to your wishes

Special people are like shining stars in your life., They make you feel happy and loved just by being themselves and letting you be your beautiful self. When you're with them, you feel safe to be real and authentic, as they accept you just the way you are.
They listen to you, laugh with you and share special moments that become cherished memories. they remind you that you are never alone and that you are valuable just by being your valuable self. always treasure them as they make your world a brighter place.

SPECIAL PEOPLE

Always accept us as we are and make us feel wondeful when we are with them

Inside of you, is a melody of laughter and adventures waiting to happen that fills your heart with priceless hopes and reminds you of what really matters.
You should sing this special song loud and clear knowing that only those kind ones can understand the music of your soul. They are the friends who make your heartbeats dance and soar above the clouds.
Cherish them and let the music that plays inside of you whenever you're together be spectacular and astounding.

Inside Your Heart

There is a beautiful song That only you and your friends can hear

If you aim high, you'll always be able to achieve incredible things. Dream big, set your goals high, and believe in yourself. With determination and hard work, you can accomplish anything you set your mind to. Every step you take towards your dreams brings you closer to reaching new heights and fulfilling your true potential. Don't be afraid to aim high because you're capable of achieving extraordinary things.

Aim High

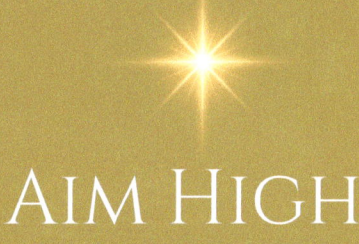

REACH FOR THE STAR, YOU NEVER KNOW WHAT FABULOUS THINGS YOU CAN ACHIEVE

Being surrounded by goodness is like being surrounded by a garden of beautiful flowers and all your favourite things.
Adorable people bring nice times to your life and make you feel happy and loved.
They listen when you need to talk, laugh with you, and share lovely moments when they are really needed.
Surrounding yourself with compassionate friends who encourage you, gives you inspiration. The more you are with them you will see that motivational things will happen and together, you'll reach greatness.

Be With Goodness

Surround yourself with people who bring you joyful times and make you feel good

Inside you lies incredible strength and courage. Believe in who you really are and your abilities, for you have the power and talent to overcome any challenge that comes your way
Even when things seem tough, remember all the times you've succeeded and how far you've come. Your determination and resilience make you a true champion.
So, hold your head high and face each day with confidence, knowing that you have what it takes to conquer anything.
Your perseverance will lead you to huge successes that you can be proud of.

You Are A Winner

WHATEVER HAPPENS THE MOST IMPORTANT THING IS THAT YOU REMEMBER YOUR STRENGTH

Being peaceful and calm is like being in a sanctuary inside your heart, everything around you becomes quieter and more placid. Take deep breaths, close your eyes and imagine a relaxing place where you feel safe and happy. Focus on the things that make you feel at ease, listening to your favourite music, spending time in nature, taking a walk, looking at the stars in the night sky.

When you practice being still and serene, it helps spread tranquility to those around you. Take time to find your inner balance and you will discover your own secret world.

Be Peaceful

When you are peaceful inside, you bring calm everywhere you go

Real beauty shines from within you, lighting up your inner world and soul, like a bright planet in the sky.
It' is not just about how you look on the outside, but it is the kindness, love and honesty you carry within you that matters the most and is what makes you extraordinary.
When you're considerate with others and show real empathy and mercy, that's when you are glowing with a magical radiance which truly sparkles for all to see.
You are beautiful, as the light you hold inside shines and illuminates every place you place your footsteps, leaving a trail of stars.

Beauty Is Within You

TRUE BEAUTY COMES FROM WITHIN YOUR HEART
AND SOUL SHINING BRIGHTLY ON EARTH

The joy of giving goes beyond just the act of sharing, it's about making a meaningful difference in someone's life.
Whether it's giving your time, helping those in need, or simply offering a sympathetic word, it allows you to connect with others with genuineness that can truly change another person's world.
It shows you that every thing we do makes a big difference and that we are all important in our own way.
Helping others not only brings gratitude to their lives but also enriches your own with a sense of accomplishment.

Joy of Giving

HELPING OTHERS BRINGS A SPECIAL KIND OF HAPPINESS THAT LASTS FOREVER

The gift of caring means showing others you value them through what you do and the efforts you make to help them make their life easier and more worthwhile.
When you care for someone, you might help them with gifts you've made, smiles you've shared or a hug of encouragement.
This makes others feel appreciated and supported and brings you a Sense of true worth and a feeling of real satisfaction.
Caring not only brightens their day but knowing you've made a difference to another person, Through showing your true self, helps plant the seeds of compassion that grow into beautiful friendships.

The gift of Caring

To show care even with the little things we do we make the world better

Expressing yourself is about sharing your thoughts, feelings and ideas with others in an open and honest way.
You can do this through words by talking or writing, or through artistic pursuits like painting, playing music, singing, or participating in activities you enjoy.
It's important to be true to yourself and communicate openly, as this helps the people you meet understand you better and builds strong and trusting relationships.
By truly showing the real wonderful you, your unique voice echoes in those who are lucky enough to meet you.

Express yourself

Feel free to sing your song and dance to your own special kind of music

The power of faith is an extraordinary force that can move mountains and bring forth miracles in your life.
With unwavering belief and trust in something greater than ourselves, we discover the ability to overcome even the biggest obstacles.
Faith fills you with hope and determination, inspiring you to persevere through challenges and pursue everything with determination.
It alights something miraculous within, propelling you to keep moving on your journey without fear, while opening the door to unexpected blessings .
When you trust a higher power, God and the angels, a fountain of endless strength appears every step of the way.

Faith moves Mountains

AN UNWAVERING BELIEF
PAVES THE WAY FOR MIRACLES TO UNFOLD